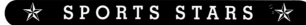
☆ SPORTS STARS ☆

FRANK THOMAS

THE BIG HURT

By Ted Cox

ℚℙ CHILDRENS PRESS ®
CHICAGO

Photo Credits

Cover, Focus on Sports; 5, ©Mitchell B. Reibel/Sports Photo Masters, Inc.; 6, Sportschrome; 9, AP/Wide World; 11, 12, Focus on Sports; 14, Reuters/ Bettmann; 17, ©Mitchell B. Reibel/Sports Photo Masters, Inc.; 19, ©Brad Newton/Sports Photo Masters, Inc.; 20, 24, Courtesy Auburn University; 26, ©Mike Haskey; 29, AP/Wide World; 30, John Swart/©Allsport USA; 33, ©Jeff Carlick/Sports Photo Masters, Inc.; 34, AP/Wide World; 37, Reuters/Bettmann; 39, AP/Wide World; 40, Focus on Sports; 43, Sportschrome; 44, ©C. Rydlewski/Sportschrome

Project Editors: Shari Joffe and Mark Friedman
Design: Beth Herman Design Associates
Photo Editor: Jan Izzo

Library of Congress Cataloging-in-Publication Data

Cox, Ted.
    Frank Thomas: the big hurt / by Ted Cox.
       p. cm. – (Sports stars)
    ISBN 0-516-04386-2
    1. Thomas, Frank, 1968- –Juvenile literature. 2. Baseball players– United States–Biography–Juvenile literature. [1. Thomas, Frank, 1968- . 2. Baseball players.] I. Title. II. Series.
GV865.T45C69   1994
796.357'092–dc20
[B]   94-9914
                                   CIP
                                   AC

FRANK THOMAS
THE BIG HURT

Frank Thomas is the most fearsome hitter in baseball. "Big Frank" stands in the batter's box at 6 feet 5 inches tall and 257 pounds. He scowls at the pitcher. He waves his bat across the plate a couple of times and then crouches as he brings his hands alongside his head. Frank is intimidating.

But what makes Frank Thomas most dangerous is how smart and patient he is. Frank won't swing at a bad pitch. Unlike most power hitters, who swing for the fences, Frank makes sure he gets a good pitch to hit — his pitch.

"Being patient is something that's easy to say, hard to do," says Frank. "But if you can do it, the pitcher eventually has to come to you.

"I'm not trying to be a bad boy when I go up there," Frank says. "I'm not taking a home-run cut every time. I don't have a home-run trot. This is my physical appearance. I worked very hard for it. But I don't play it up.

"Not many guys in this game have ever been able to hit for average, for power, and drive in runs," he adds. "I'd like to combine all those things. I'd like to do things that no one has ever done before. I don't want to be just a good hitter. I want to be great."

Frank, the first baseman for the Chicago White Sox, is already on the road to the Hall of Fame. He was named the Most Valuable Player in the American League in only his third full season. In each of those years, he batted over .300, with more than 20 home runs, 100 RBI, 100 runs scored, and 100 walks. Frank made it seem routine, but it has been four decades since anyone put up those numbers three years in a row. The last one to do it, Ted Williams, is the hitter to whom Frank is most often compared.

--- ★ ★ ★ ---

"If you could chisel out a hitter who only swings at what he can hit, it's Frank," says White Sox batting coach Walt Hriniak. "Someone once said to me, 'If there's anything negative about Frank, it's that he's too selective.' My response was, 'They said the same thing about Ted Williams.'"

"In my 30 years in this game I have never seen anyone like him," says Ken "Hawk" Harrelson, a former baseball star and now a TV announcer for the White Sox. "In another 30 years we may be talking about Frank Thomas in the same way we talk about Ted Williams."

Harrelson is the one who came up with Frank's nickname — The Big Hurt. "I really like it," says Frank, with one of his big smiles. "It's the first nickname I've really liked. And it really explains what I try to do with the baseball every time."

Big Frank is a menacing sight whether he's at bat or in the field.

With the help of the eye black Frank wears on his cheeks, he looks as fierce as his nickname. Players put black under their eyes to cut down on the glare from the sun. But for Frank it has another purpose. "The eye black is my war paint," he says. "When I put it on, it's time to go to war."

Off the field, Frank is friendly and happy. But on the field, he is completely different. "Nobody will ever demand more of Frank than Frank does," says Tim Raines, his best friend on the White Sox. "He's like Dr. Jeykll and Mr. Hyde. Off the field he's sweet and nice. On the field, well, you should hear some of the things he says about himself after a strikeout."

"I love this game, but when it's time to work it's time to work," says Frank. "That's the approach I've had all my life.

"There [are] no short cuts to success in this business. You've got to be disciplined, you've got to be motivated, and you've really got to bust your tail."

It hasn't been easy, not even for a player as big and talented as Frank. He faced many disappointments on his way to the big leagues, but each time he used those disappointments to make himself work harder. He says, "I guess you could say a lot of little hurts went into making the Big Hurt."

Frank was born May 27, 1968, in Columbus, Georgia, the fifth child of Charlie Mae and Frank Thomas, Sr. Frank's father was a bail bondsman and a deacon in the local Baptist church; his mother was a textile worker.

Frank was always big for his age. By the time he was 10, he was a slugging center fielder on a Little League team. Even then, pitchers were afraid of him. "Kids would throw the ball behind him, over the backstop, all over the place," says Frank Sr. "They'd do anything to avoid pitching to him."

Baseball, football, basketball — Frank played them all, but he especially loved basketball. Whatever the season, he'd spend six or seven hours a day playing ball. "I never had to worry about him," says Frank Sr. "It didn't matter what time of day or night it was, I knew Frank was at the Boys Club or the playground, somewhere with a ball in his hands."

Frank's father always knew his son was playing sports and keeping out of trouble.

★ ★ ★

Frank couldn't hide his disappointment when he was cut from the Columbus High School baseball team as a freshman. He felt he was good enough, but the coaches thought he was too young. So Frank devoted himself more than ever to baseball in the next year. In his sophomore season, he not only made the team, he hit .478 and led Columbus to the state title. Fighting back from disappointment would become a pattern with Frank.

It was then that Frank developed his keen batting eye. "I was a free swinger when I was younger," he says. But his high-school baseball coach, Bobby Howard, tutored him with a demanding lesson: every time Frank swung at a bad pitch, he had to run laps.

"I learned the hard way," Frank says. "Either you've got to do it the right way or you're going to be a tired young man."

Ever since high school, Frank has worked long and hard to perfect his swing.

Frank as an Auburn University football player

★ ★ ★

Frank was an all-city athlete in baseball, football, and basketball. He was all-state in baseball and was named the local Player of the Year his senior season. When the major-league baseball draft was held that summer, 888 players were chosen—but not Frank. He had already accepted a football scholarship at Auburn University in Georgia, where he would also get to play baseball. But Frank says that if he had been drafted by a baseball team, he would have signed a contract "in a heartbeat."

"I couldn't believe no one would take a chance on me," he says. "I basically played college football because football was my only choice. But I was grateful for a football scholarship. And, looking back, it was probably a blessing that it happened that way."

"Playing football for Auburn was a whole new world for me. It made me a man." To this day, Frank says his two strongest influences in sports were his high-school baseball coach, Bobby Howard, and Auburn football coach Pat Dye. As a college freshman, he played tight end on an Auburn team that ended the season among the top 10 in the nation. The coaches said he had the potential to be All-Pro in the National Football League.

"I had always thought I was working hard. But [in college football], I learned what hard work means. Just to be competitive, I had to really throw the weights around," Frank says. "When I showed up for baseball practice that spring, I could tell my power had doubled.

I told the baseball coaches, 'I'm going to make an impact on your club.' And they laughed. They thought it was kind of cute, coming from this little freshman football player."

Frank quickly convinced his coaches with his bat. With the first ball he hit in spring practice, Frank almost knocked down the shortstop with a line drive. He went on to a stunning freshman season, setting a university record with 21 homers. He was also named a Southeastern Conference all-star.

Frank was forced to give up basketball because of problems with his ankles. Then he suffered a knee injury in practice before the fall football season. That was the end of his days as a multi-sport star. Frank decided to concentrate on baseball and preserve his health.

Frank eventually gave up his other sports and starred in baseball at Auburn.

The next spring, he led the conference in batting average and was named the starting first baseman on the conference all-star team. He made the United States National Team that summer — but then he was cut from the squad before the Olympics.

"I couldn't believe it," says Frank. "It was a constant battle to prove myself in baseball."

And he kept getting better and better. In his junior year, he hit an astounding .403 and was named the conference's most valuable player. The Chicago White Sox were convinced. They picked Frank seventh in the 1989 draft. He finished his career at Auburn with the school records for homers, RBI, extra-base hits, total bases, and on-base percentage.

**Frank didn't even log a full season in the minors before the
White Sox called him up.**

Before 1990 spring training, the White Sox decided that Frank would go to AA Birmingham — two steps away from the majors. But Frank was determined to make it to the top. He remembers, "I dominated that spring. I hammered the ball. I showed them I was ready for the big leagues." He hit .529 in spring training, but the Sox stuck to their decision and sent him to Birmingham for more seasoning.

On the way north from spring training, Frank stopped in Columbus to talk with his father. "He was hurt," says Frank Sr., "really hurt. But he was going up there dedicated to working hard and being ready."

Frank took out his hurt feelings on the
AA pitchers. In just over 100 games, he hit 18
homers and drove in 71 runs. He had 112 walks
and was hitting .323 when finally the Sox had
seen enough. They called him up on August 2.
They were in a pennant race, and they needed
all the help they could get.

Frank made an impression the moment
he reported to the White Sox. Even though
he had skipped AAA, Frank's batting average
actually rose in the majors. He put together
a 13-game hitting streak and was named
American League Player of the Week in
September. The Sox finished second in the
Western Division, but Frank finished at .330,
with seven homers and 31 RBI—in just a third
of a season. He had arrived.

Frank as a major-league rookie

In 1991, Frank created a sensation in his first full season in the majors. He hit 32 homers and drove in 109 runs (fifth in the league in both categories) while batting .318. He also led the league with 138 walks and a .453 on-base percentage. The Sox again came in second, but Frank came in third in MVP voting. In his first full season, he was already recognized as one of the best players in the league.

Frank had done all that while suffering from a shoulder injury. He couldn't throw well, so he was the designated hitter more than he played first base. He had minor surgery after the season and returned to the field in 1992.

It wasn't an easy transition. In 1992, Frank made 13 errors — a lot for a first baseman. His defensive problems took the shine off another great year at the plate: .323 batting average, 24 home runs, and 115 RBI. Frank became the first player in almost 40 years and just the eighth player in baseball history to bat .300 with 20 homers, 100 RBI, 100 runs, and 100 walks in back-to-back seasons. Yet the White Sox slipped to third, and Frank fell to eighth in MVP balloting.

"To be honest," Frank says, "I used to stand out there on defense and think about hitting." But he also knew that in the major leagues, he absolutely had to play in the field. So Frank went back to work.

In 1992, defense was the only flaw in Frank's game, but he worked hard and cut down on his errors.

That winter, he returned to the gym for the first time since college. And when spring training came, he worked hard in the field taking grounders. He'd show up at the park early in the morning to start practice. "I like to go out there and work hard," he says. "I really feel I'm a blue-collar player."

When the 1993 season started, that hard work paid off. At first base, Frank was much improved. And at the plate he had more power than ever. He mashed 41 homers and led the White Sox to the top of their division.

Most power hitters bat cleanup — fourth in the lineup. But Frank likes to bat third. With his high on-base percentage, that means he can not only drive in the first two batters, he can get on base for the cleanup hitter. Babe Ruth, another great hitter who knew how to draw a walk, also usually hit third. And batting third means Frank always gets to hit in the first inning.

As the Sox kept winning in 1993, one of the keys was that Frank was giving them early leads. He hit 15 first-inning homers that year. "I call them my school bells," Frank says. "The offense is in session.

"I want to be known as the guy who's clutch, who's not afraid to go to the plate with men on, a guy who delivers." With Frank in that role, the Sox won the Western Division title.

In the League Championship Series, however, Frank was denied the chance to produce in the clutch. The Toronto Blue Jays' pitchers walked Frank whenever they could. Frank knows that in many situations, a walk is as good as a hit. If he gets on base and scores a run, that's as good as him driving in a run. But his teammates didn't come through. Frank homered in the fourth game to help the Sox tie the series, but the Jays went on to win the playoffs, as well as the World Series.

Frank's best friends on the 1993 White Sox were Tim Raines (center) and Bo Jackson (right). Frank and Bo played football together at Auburn University.

After the disappointment of losing in the playoffs wore off, Frank and his teammates realized that it had been a great season. The Sox had developed a superb young pitching staff that would surely keep them in contention for years. And Frank had firmly established himself as one of the great hitters of his generation. His 41 home runs in 1993 were a new White Sox record and placed him second in the American League. He also finished second in RBI (128), and sixth in batting (.317). And the biggest honor came early that winter: Frank was the unanimous choice for American League MVP, only the eighth unanimous MVP in history.

It was a big prize to capture, but Frank still wasn't entirely pleased. "I'm the kind of guy who would rather win a championship than get MVP," says Frank. "I'm the kind of guy who understands there are no shortcuts to success."

Frank and his wife Elise are all smiles as "The Big Hurt" accepts the 1993 American League MVP award.

With his amazing ability and his big smile, Frank is becoming one of the most popular athletes in sports. At the end of his MVP season, he signed a new contract giving him $7 million a season. He became second-highest-paid baseball player, behind Barry Bonds. But he's trying not to let the attention change his life. He tries to live a normal life in the Chicago suburbs with his wife, Elise, and their two children.

"I'm still as open to people as I've always been," says Frank. "It's not uncommon for me to meet someone in the store and say, 'Hello, how ya doing?' and then start talking to them. Then people find out who I am and ask why I would want to talk to them, a nobody. I don't believe that."

Frank is also active in many charities, especially the Leukemia Society of America. Frank's younger sister died from leukemia when she was 2 1/2 years old. "I was 11 at the time and her favorite person," he says. "It really hurt me. Those are things I build off. Coming from a poor family, I can relate to everything.

"I believe I can do some things that have never been done before, and that's why I'm working as hard as ever," he says. "I want to be a great ballplayer. I want to be a Hall of Famer."

Frank already is well on his way.

Chronology

1968 – Frank Edward Thomas is born to Frank Thomas, Sr., and Charlie Mae Thomas on May 27, 1968, in Columbus, Georgia.

1983-86 – Frank is a three-sport star at Columbus High School, all-city in baseball, basketball, and football. As a senior, Frank is named the local Player of the Year in baseball and is all-state. He signs a football scholarship at Auburn University that also allows for him to play baseball.

1986 – Frank plays tight end for the Auburn football team and catches three passes.

1987 – Frank sets an Auburn baseball record with 21 homers and is named to *Baseball America* magazine's all-freshman team and to the All-Southeastern Conference team.
– He quits football after suffering knee injury in practice.

1988 – Frank leads the SEC with a .385 batting average.
– He is a member of the U.S. National Team, but is cut before Olympics.

1989 – Frank is named SEC MVP, leading the conference with a .403 batting average and 83 RBI; he finishes second in the conference with 19 homers.
– He is chosen number seven in the first round of the major-league free-agent draft by the Chicago White Sox.
– Frank completes his college career as the Auburn leader in homers, RBI, extra-base hits, total bases, and on-base percentage. Joins White Sox rookie-league team and is promoted to Class A.

1990 – Frank hits .529 in spring training but is assigned to Class AA Birmingham. Hits .323 with 18 homers, 71 RBI, and 112 walks in 109 games before being called up to Sox.
– In just 60 games with the White Sox, Frank hits .330 with 7 homers and 31 RBI.

1991 – Frank hits .318 with 32 homers and 109 RBI in his first full season in the majors. He leads the American League in walks (138) and on-base percentage (.453).

– Finishes third in MVP balloting, behind Cal Ripken and Cecil Fielder.

1992 – Frank hits .323 with 24 homers and 115 RBI. Leads American League in extra-base hits (72) and in on-base percentage (.439). Ties for league lead in walks (122) and doubles (46). Becomes only the eighth AL player to hit .300 with 20 homers, 100 RBI, 100 runs scored, and 100 walks in consecutive seasons (the others are Babe Ruth, Lou Gehrig, Mel Ott, Jimmie Foxx, Hank Greenberg, Ted Williams, and Stan Musial — all Hall of Famers).

1993 – Frank hits .317 with 41 homers and 128 RBI in leading Sox to American League West title.

– Wins the AL MVP Award in a unanimous vote, becoming only eighth AL player to do so.

– Signs contract extension worth more than $7 million a year, making him second-highest-paid player behind Barry Bonds.

★ ★ ★

About the Author

Ted Cox is a Chicago journalist who works at the *Daily Southtown*. He has covered sports for the *Chicago Reader* and *Chicago* magazine. He worked at United Press International and holds a B.S. in journalism from the University of Illinois at Urbana-Champaign. He lives in Chicago with his wife, Catherine, and their daughter, Sadie.